Contents

Any words appearing in the text in bold, **like this**,
are explained in the glossary.

Where in the sky is Mercury?

You do not have to look high in the sky to see Mercury. Look towards the **horizon** instead. About an hour before sunrise or after sunset, you can see Mercury – the planet closest to the Sun. It is not very big, but it glows. Sometimes another, larger planet such as Venus can be seen near by. If you look for Venus first, it will be easier to find Mercury.

When can I see Mercury?

You can only see Mercury a few times every **year.** This is partly because Mercury is closer to the Sun than any other planet in our **solar system.** The light from the Sun makes it difficult to see Mercury. Think about what happens when someone shines a bright light in your eyes. It is hard to see anything. The same thing happens

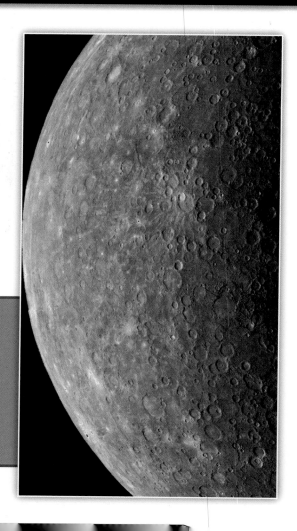

This was one of the first photos taken of Mercury. The side that we see here is the side that was facing towards the Sun at that time.

when a fielder in cricket "loses" a ball in the Sun. The **glare** makes it difficult for the player to see the ball. Because Mercury is so close to the Sun, it is easy to "lose" Mercury in the Sun's glare. For that reason, the best time to view Mercury is when it is far away from the Sun in the sky.

Of the eight planets in our solar system, Mercury is closest to the Sun.

The solar system

The solar system is made of everything that circles the Sun: planets, **comets**, **asteroids**, and other objects. The Sun's **gravity** pulls on all of the objects in our solar system. If it were not for the pull of the Sun, the planets would travel in straight lines. This would send them out into deep space! The force of gravity keeps Mercury and the other planets in regular paths around the Sun, called **orbits.**

Sometimes Mercury looks like our Moon

Mercury has **phases** just like Earth's Moon. When Mercury is between Earth and the Sun, it has a thin shape like a sliver of the Moon. When Mercury is furthest from the Sun, we can see about half of the sunlit side of the planet's surface. It appears to be "half full". A "full" Mercury appears when the Sun is directly between Earth and Mercury, but we cannot see this because the Sun's **glare** is now too bright.

Mercury looks a lot like the Earth's Moon, with thousands of craters where **asteroids** hit the planet.

Who found Mercury?

People have known about Mercury since ancient times because they did not need a **telescope** to see it. They were able to see the planet in the night sky, even though Mercury is the smallest planet in the **solar system**. In addition to its small size, Mercury is hard to study because the Sun's glare makes it difficult to observe the planet for long periods.

How did Mercury get its name?

The Romans had a messenger god named Mercury, whom they believed had wings on his sandals for speed. Because the planet Mercury moved so quickly through the sky, Roman astronomers named it after their fast-moving god.

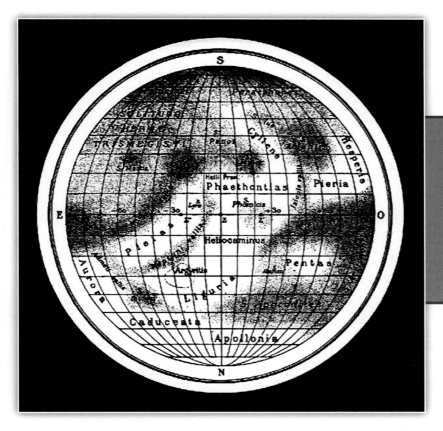

This 1920s map of Mercury was based on what astronomers of that time knew about the planet.

Astronomers in the late 1700s and late 1800s used telescopes to look at Mercury. They saw dark patches on the planet, but they did not know they were looking at **craters**. Italian astronomer Giovanni Schiaparelli saw markings on the planet's surface.

The further away a planet is from the Sun, the larger its orbit has to be.

How long is Mercury's year?

Mercury's **orbit** is the smallest of all the planets because it is so close to the Sun. The speedy little planet travels 48 kilometres (30 miles) per second. Earth travels only 30 kilometres (19 miles) per second. It takes Mercury only 88 Earth **days** to complete one **revolution**, (circle) around the Sun. That means Mercury's **year** is 88 Earth days.

Mercury days are very long

As they move through the sky, all planets spin around on their **axis**: the imaginary line through the centre of a planet from its north pole to its south pole. The time it takes to complete one **rotation** around the axis is what we call a day.

An Earth day lasts about 24 hours. On Earth, one rotation equals one day. Mercury spins very slowly on its axis. It takes an amazing 59 Earth days for Mercury to complete one rotation. After Mercury rotates once, the Sun does not rise again. Why do you think this happens?

Why are days on Mercury so long?

Like Earth, Mercury moves around the Sun while it rotates, but Mercury moves much, much faster. By the time Mercury completes one rotation on its axis in 59 days, it has moved a lot further through its 88-day orbit and changed its position to the Sun. That means the Sun is not in the right position to "rise" in the "morning" of Mercury's day. Mercury has to spin around three times, while it makes two orbits, before the Sun will rise again on Mercury. If you were to stand on the surface of Mercury to see a sunrise, you would have to wait a full Mercury year – 88-day orbit – to see the sunset. You would have to wait another 88 days to see the next sunrise.

This is an artist's idea of what Mercury and the Sun look like together.

What's special about Mercury?

If you got lost on Mercury, you could use a **compass**. Of the four planets closest to the Sun, only Mercury and Earth have **magnetic fields**. Mercury's magnetic field is much weaker than Earth's. Still, if you were hiking on Mercury and got lost, a compass could show you which direction was north. Like Earth, Mercury acts like a huge magnet that is lined up in a north-south direction. The pointer on a magnetic compass would line up the same way. This is evidence that Mercury may have a **molten core**.

Scientists use radio telescopes, such as this one in Puerto Rico, to study Mercury and the other planets.

There might be frozen water on Mercury

Scientists use **radio telescopes** to bounce **radar** waves off the planet Mercury. They have found that there are places on Mercury that reflect radar in the same way that ice does. The presence of ice would be strange, though, because Mercury is so close to the Sun and is a very hot planet.

Where is the ice?

There are **craters** on Mercury, even at its north and south poles. Some of the craters are very deep. The planet's **axis** is very straight and not tilted like Earth's. The Sun shining from the side of the planet never reaches the bottoms of the craters near the poles. These craters might be deep enough and cold enough for ice to form.

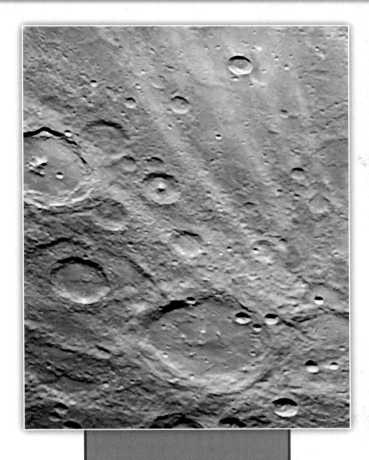

The largest crater in this picture of Mercury's surface is about 100 kilometres (62 miles) across.

Where did the water come from?

One theory for where the water on Mercury came from is that the **comets** that crashed into Mercury long ago might have contained water. When they hit the planet, the comets could have released water, which then froze into ice. Another, less likely, theory is that water from the interior of the planet came up to the surface. If water came up into the cold bottom of a **crater**, it would have frozen into ice.

No one has seen the ice on Mercury, and there are no pictures of it yet. So far, scientists only have theories about the ice. The bottoms of the craters are too dark to photograph. Scientists have collected **data** that they compare to data from other places where they know there is ice. Since the data is similar, they can say that ice probably exists on Mercury.

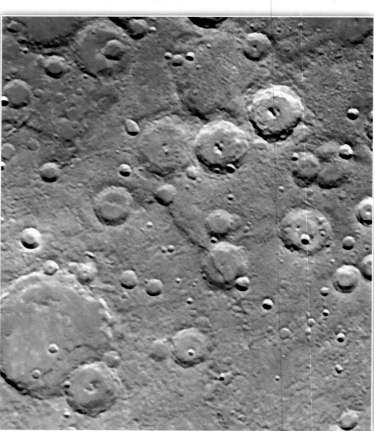

This part of the planet's surface has a large number of craters clustered together.

How's the weather on Mercury?

It gets very hot on Mercury, as you would expect on a planet that is so close to the Sun. The hottest daytime temperatures can reach 427°C (800°F). The coldest temperatures, which are in areas facing away from the Sun as Mercury rotates, can drop as low as –184°C (–300°F). This is a temperature range of more than 600 degrees. No other planet has such a wide temperature range. The average daily temperature on Mercury is about 370°C (700°F).

If Mercury is so close to the Sun, how could anywhere on the planet get so cold?

Mercury has almost no **atmosphere**. An atmosphere on a planet is like a coat on a person. The atmosphere keeps the temperatures from ranging widely. Mercury's atmosphere is so thin that it is barely there at all. Because the atmosphere is so thin, the planet has a wide range of temperatures. Its high temperatures are 1,000 degrees higher than its low temperatures.

Mercury's atmosphere is so thin that it is invisible. If a person were to look up at the sky from the surface of the planet, the sky would be black.

You could not get a breath of fresh air

Spacecraft and **telescopes** on the Earth have detected helium, oxygen, and sodium in Mercury's very thin **atmosphere**. Other gases that have been found in even smaller amounts are hydrogen, potassium, and calcium. This is completely different from the air we breathe on Earth, which is mostly nitrogen mixed with some oxygen. There is only ever about a tonne of oxygen in Mercury's atmosphere. This is trillions of times less than the oxygen there is on Earth.

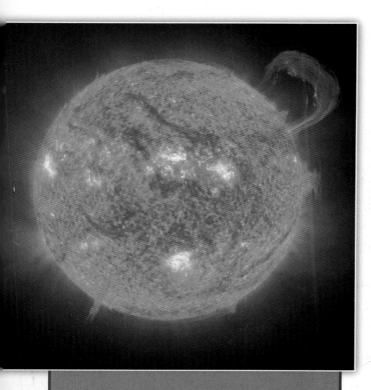

The Sun's very hot atmosphere creates a solar wind that affects the planets.

Scientists think that the oxygen and sodium in Mercury's atmosphere come from the surface of the planet. Oxygen and sodium atoms are either knocked off the surface by very small **meteorites** or by **solar wind**. They may also **evaporate** from the surface because of the high temperatures.

The helium in Mercury's atmosphere is blown there by solar wind. All the gases in Mercury's atmosphere escape quickly because of the planet's low **gravity** and high temperatures.

There are no seasons on Mercury

On Earth, it is summer on the part of Earth that is tilted towards the Sun. When the tilt of Earth's **axis** turns a part of Earth away from the Sun, it is winter. Mercury's axis is almost straight up and down. As a result, Mercury does not have seasons like Earth does.

Why is Mercury so small?

Mercury, the second smallest planet in our **solar system**, is less than half as wide as Earth. Its nearness to the Sun may be part of the reason for Mercury's small size. When the planets were first formed, from gas and bits of dust floating in space, the Sun had already formed. That was about 4.6 billion years ago. The Sun's heat and solar winds overpowered Mercury's gravity as the planet's gravity tried to pull in dust particles. Planets further from the Sun did not have these problems. As a result, all of the planets except Pluto are much bigger than Mercury.

The bright side of the planet is the side on which the Sun is shining. The darker side is the side on which the Sun is not shining.

What would I see if I went to Mercury?

Scientists found out much of what they know about Mercury's surface from pictures taken by the **fly-by** mission of the *Mariner 10* space probe. They now know that Mercury has many, many **craters.** Its surface looks a lot like our Moon's surface. One reason for all the craters is Mercury's thin **atmosphere. Meteorites** and **asteroids** do not burn up as they approach the surface of Mercury as they might do in a thick atmosphere. Most of them crash right into the planet.

Craters on Mercury vary in size. They can be the size of a football pitch or more than 1,287 kilometres (800 miles) wide. Sometimes there are craters inside the craters. At the bottom of the craters there may be smooth **plains** and peaks. The craters and other landforms on Mercury are covered with a mixture of fine dust and sand. Craters are one characteristic of the Rocky Planets, which include Mercury, Venus, Earth, and Mars.

This false-colour image was made from a series of pictures placed side by side. The bright yellow stripe is not a feature of the planet. It is a gap between the pictures.

What could make such a big crater?

Scientists think that a large meteorite or asteroid crashed into Mercury about 4 billion years ago. It was so large that when it hit Mercury, it must have made the entire planet shake. Mercury probably shook so much that its surface cracked in many places.

This is an artist's view of what asteroids look like while travelling through outer space.

The Caloris Basin

One of the largest **impact craters** in the **solar system** is on Mercury. It is called the Caloris Basin. A **meteorite** hitting the planet made this long, bowl-shaped hole. The Caloris Basin is about 1,300 kilometres (800 miles) wide. It is so big that you could put the entire country of France in it!

The bottom of the **crater** has smooth **plains** dotted with shallow craters. The craters were made after the Caloris Basin

formed. There are also ridges sticking up. Scientists think that the Caloris Basin was flooded with **lava** a long time ago. This made the inside surface flatter and smoother. A ring of mountains circles the outside part of the Caloris Basin. These mountains are about 1.6 kilometres (1 mile) high. Scientists only know for certain what half of the crater looks like. When *Mariner 10* flew by the Caloris Basin in the 1970s, half of it was in darkness.

The floor of the Caloris Basin is covered with ridges and cracks.

How did the Caloris Basin get its name?

The word "caloris" comes from the Latin word *calor*, which means "heat". The Caloris Basin is the hottest place on Mercury. Temperatures in the Caloris Basin get as high as 427°C (800°F).

There are smooth hills and domes between the **scarps** (cliffs) in the Caloris Basin.

An area on the opposite side of Mercury from the Caloris Basin was shaped by the impact of the meteorite. **Seismic waves** from the impact, similar to an earthquake, were focused in these areas and caused the surface to crack. The shock waves also caused some areas on Mercury's surface to sink. In other areas, the waves pushed up hills on the surface.

The smooth plains

No **volcanoes** have been found on Mercury, but there may have been some long ago. Some areas of Mercury are large, smooth **plains**. Scientists think these plains may have formed when volcanoes **erupted**. The **lava** from each volcano would have covered the ground like a layer of syrup. When the lava cooled, the ground would be smoother and flatter.

Volcanoes such as this one in Hawaii show us how lava flows during an eruption.

Other scientists think some of the smooth plains might have formed when **molten** rock from the impact of huge **meteorites** splashed up and fell back on to the surface. Over many years, this sheet of molten rock cooled and smoothed out the ground to form plains. On the half of Mercury that has been photographed, the plains are in one area and most of the **craters** are in another area.

The steep cliffs

Photos of Mercury show many long lines across its surface. These lines are high, steep cliffs called **scarps**. The largest known scarp on Mercury is the Discovery Rupes. It is more than 500 kilometres (300 miles) long and 3 kilometres (2 miles) high.

Scientists think some of these scarps may have been pushed up as the planet was squeezed (compressed). What would cause this?

One theory is that as Mercury's **core** cooled and shrank, the surface land had to fit on a smaller area and was pushed upwards. This may have caused the distance around Mercury to get smaller by about 1 to 2 kilometres (0.5 to 1 mile).

This photograph shows a close-up view of the Discovery Rupes scarp on Mercury.

What is inside Mercury?

In the very centre of all planets is the **core**. Mercury's core is about 3,700 kilometres (2,300 miles) across. That distance is about as far as the United States is wide. The core is made mostly of iron. There are also small amounts of metal called nickel. Mercury's core makes up a large part of the planet. In fact, in relation to the size of the planet, Mercury's core is larger than any other planet's core in our **solar system**.

Scientists think that part of Mercury's core may be **molten.** The iron in that part of the core would be melted and soft. Scientific **data** suggests that Earth's **magnetic field** is created by the movement of molten materials in the outer part of the planet's core. Perhaps Mercury's magnetic field is created in the same way.

This artwork shows where the crust, mantle, and core may begin and end inside the planet Mercury.

The mantle

Outside of the core is the **mantle**. Mercury's mantle is about 560 kilometres (350 miles) thick. You would have to drive for about six hours on a motorway to travel that far. Scientists think Mercury's mantle is made of **silicate** materials. Silicate materials are combinations of the **element** silicon and other elements, such as aluminum or iron. In natural conditions, silicon is always found combined with other elements. Earth's **crust** contains silicon combined with oxygen.

The crust

The outside layer of the planet Mercury is called the crust. Most of Mercury's crust is very old. It probably formed about 4.2 billion years ago, burying any **craters** from **meteorite** impacts long before that time. The smooth **plains** on the surface of the crust are younger. They are only about 3.8 billion years old.

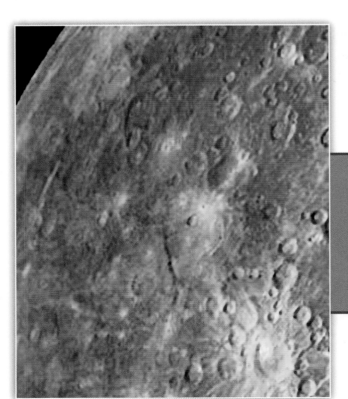

In this image, colour filters were used to show scientists the different materials found in Mercury's crust.

Could I ever go to Mercury?

As far as space travel goes, it would not take you too long to get to Mercury. The exact travel time would depend on how close or how far Mercury is from Earth as the two planets **orbit** the Sun. You would also have to plan the trip so that you can catch up to Mercury, which is orbiting the Sun much faster than Earth. Every 116 Earth **days**, Mercury zooms past Earth.

Since Mercury is so close to the Sun, you will need a space suit that can keep you cool in the extreme heat of 427°C (800°F). The same suit will also need to keep you warm when temperatures drop to their lowest levels of −183°C (−361°F).

It would be a good idea to spend most of your time at the poles. Mercury's **axis** is almost straight up and down, so the poles do not get as much sunlight and it is not as hot there. The ice at the bottom of the **craters** could provide drinking water.

Mariner 10 was launched in November 1973 on its mission to explore Venus and Mercury.

Since water is made of hydrogen and oxygen, oxygen could be processed out of the water to help refill oxygen tanks. You would need an oxygen tank to breathe on Mercury.

A visit to Mercury by astronauts would have to be far in the future. **Radio telescopes** that use **radar** have provided most of the information we have about Mercury. One space mission has flown by Mercury, but no space probe has landed on the planet.

Colour has been added to this image to show the view of Mercury from *Mariner 10*.

How does radar astronomy work?

Scientists send radio waves to Mercury. The waves are made up of individual **radar** signals. It takes about four minutes for a signal travelling at the speed of light to reach Mercury when it is closest to Earth. Scientists record how long it takes the signal to bounce back. Then they compare the times for signals that bounced off different parts of Mercury. If a signal took more time, travelling a longer distance, it probably went to the bottom of a deep **crater**. If the signal took less time, travelling a shorter distance, it probably hit high ground or a mountain.

This is the radar system for a powerful camera used by NASA.

The Mariner mission to Mercury

Of the 10 *Mariner* missions, only *Mariner 10* (the last one) went to Mercury. The National Aeronautics and Space Administration (NASA) launched it on 3 November 1973. The spacecraft flew past Venus three months later. After taking pictures of Venus, *Mariner 10* carried on to Mercury. It flew past Mercury twice in 1974 and once in 1975, with six months between each **fly-by.** *Mariner 10* took about 10,000 photographs. Only about half of Mercury was photographed because every time *Mariner* returned to the planet the same side was always in the dark.

Future missions

NASA launched the *Messenger* mission to Mercury in 2004. After three fly-bys, the spacecraft will **orbit** Mercury in 2011.

The European Space Agency (ESA) is working with Japan to launch another mission, *BepiColombo*, that will arrive in 2019. Scientists hope that both missions will give us more information about Mercury's **crust**, how the surface was formed, the thin **atmosphere**, and the **magnetic field**.

The *Messenger* spacecraft began its 8 billion kilometre (5 billion mile) journey to Mercury in 2004.

Fact File

	MERCURY	EARTH
Average distance from the Sun	58 million kilometres (36 million miles)	150 million kilometres (93 million miles)
Revolution around the Sun	88 Earth **days**	1 Earth **year** (365 days)
Average speed of orbit	48 kilometres/second (30 miles/second)	30 kilometres/second (18.6 miles/second)
Diameter at equator	4,876 kilometres (3,030 miles)	12,756 kilometres (7,926 miles)
Time for one rotation	59 Earth days	24 hours
Atmosphere	oxygen, sodium, helium	nitrogen, oxygen
Moons	0	1
Temperature range	–183°C (–361°F) to 427°C (800°F)	–69°C (–92°F) to 58°C (136°F)

The *Mariner 10* spacecraft, shown here, gathered much of the information we have about the planet Mercury.

A trip to Mercury from Earth

- When Mercury and Earth come closest to each other in their **orbits**, they are 77 million kilometres (48 million miles) apart.

- Travelling to Mercury by car at 113 kilometres (70 miles) per hour would take at least 88 years.

- Travelling to Mercury by rocket at 11 kilometres (7 miles) per second would take at least 79 days.

Near the centre of this photograph is a fresh **crater** inside an older crater. The **meteorite** impacts that caused the two craters must have happened at different times.

More interesting facts

- Your weight on Mercury would be just over a third of your weight on Earth. This is because of the difference in **gravity** on the two planets.

- On Mercury, sunshine is more than six times brighter than it is on Earth. This is because Mercury is much closer to the Sun.

- Light from the Sun takes only about three minutes to reach Mercury.

Glossary

asteroid large piece of floating rock that formed at the same time the planets formed

astronomer person who studies objects in outer space

atmosphere all of the gases that surround an object in outer space

axis imaginary line through the centre of an object in space, around which it spins as it rotates

comet ball of ice and rock that orbits the Sun

compass magnetic tool used to measure direction

core material at the centre of a planet

crater bowl-shaped hole in the ground that is made by a meteorite or a burst of lava

crust top, solid layer of an object in outer space. The outer part of the crust is called the surface.

data scientific information

day time it takes for a planet to spin around its axis once (another word for "rotation")

element basic substance

erupt explode or spill out

evaporate lose all moisture and turn into vapour or steam

fly-by mission to a planet in which the spacecraft does not land

glare uncomfortably bright light

gravity invisible force that pulls objects towards the centre of an object in outer space

horizon part of Earth where the sky and land appear to meet

impact crater bowl-shaped hole in the ground that is made by a meteorite

lava melted rock from inside a planet or moon that pours out on to the surface

magnetic field region in which the motion of electrical particles and magnets is affected. It protects a planet from the wind of electrical particles coming from the Sun.

mantle middle layer of a planet or moon. It lies between the core and the crust.

meteorite piece of rock or dust that lands on the surface of a planet or a moon from space

molten melted into liquid form by high temperatures

orbit curved path of one object in space moving around another object. We say "Earth orbits (moves around) the Sun."

phase changing appearance of a moon or planet as it rotates. The phase is shaped by the amount of the sunlit side of the object that can be seen by the viewer.

plain flat area of land

radar method of studying objects in which sound waves are bounced off an object and back to a machine

radio telescope machine that collects information by sending and receiving radar signals

revolution time it takes for a planet to travel once around the Sun (also known as a year)

rotation time it takes for a planet to spin on its axis once (also known as a day)

scarp steep slope or cliff on the surface of a Rocky Planet

seismic wave shock wave caused by an impact; similar to an earthquake

silicate combination of the element silicon and other elements such as aluminum or iron

solar system group of objects in outer space that all float in orbits around a central star

solar wind material continually coming off the Sun's surface and travelling through space

telescope instrument used by astronomers to study objects in outer space

volcano mountain built up from layers of hardened lava

year time it takes for a planet to orbit the Sun once (another word for "revolution")

More books to read

Mercury, Carlo P. Croce (Rosen Publishing Group, 2005)

Mercury, Salvatore Tocci (Children's Press, 2006)

Stargazers' Guides: Can We Travel to the Stars?, Rosalind Mist and Andrew Solway (Heinemann Library, 2006)

Index